Unstoppable Woman

12 Power Moves to Create a Life You Love and Achieve the Success You Deserve

by

Marsha Lynn Hudson, EdS

Introduction

Unstoppable Woman: 12 Power Moves to Create a Life You Love and Achieve the Success You Deserve is a journey through your own potential, designed to help you awaken to all that you are capable of, and to inspire you to step boldly into the life you truly want. This is a letter from one woman to another—from me, who has felt the call of more, to you, who may be feeling that same stirring in your soul. Each chapter is crafted to guide you into a new realm of possibility, blending wisdom, real-life stories, actionable strategies, and warm encouragement.

These "Power Moves" aren't just concepts; they're steps you can start taking today. From discovering your core values and setting goals with heart to building resilience and crafting a vision for a fulfilling future, each chapter gives you tools to make real changes that align with your truest desires. Together, we'll move through fear, self-doubt, and limiting beliefs, replacing them with a foundation of confidence, joy, and self-worth. You'll come out of this journey empowered, with a clear path to the success and fulfillment that have always been waiting for you.

Whether you're looking to ignite a new chapter, build confidence, or finally give yourself permission to pursue your dreams, this book is for you. Here, you'll find the strength, courage, and motivation to embrace your own unstoppable power.

- **Get your pen and highlighter for this book. You will want to mark this book, make notes in this book, highlight words in this book, and make this book your success roadmap!**

Commitment to Self

"I commit to honoring my journey and embracing my power. As I read this book, I promise to show up for myself fully, with an open heart and a willingness to grow.

I will take each step toward cultivating the unstoppable woman within me. I am worthy of success, peace, and joy, and I will prioritize my well-being, my goals, and my dreams.

I am committed to taking the actions needed to transform my life, and I trust that every chapter will guide me closer to the person I am meant to be. This is my time, and I am ready to become unstoppable."

Signed:

____

Description

Unstoppable Woman: 12 Power Moves to Create a Life You Love and Achieve the Success You Deserve is more than just a self-help book—it's an empowering guide for women who are ready to break free from limitations and step into their fullest potential. Written with warmth, authenticity, and a deep belief in the power of women, this book is a call to action for anyone who's ready to live on their own terms and create a life they can be proud of.

Inside, you'll discover 12 transformative "Power Moves" that will take you through a journey of self-discovery, personal growth, and practical strategies to help you achieve lasting success. Each move is carefully designed to speak to the heart and mind of the modern woman, with a focus on clarity, purpose, and actionable steps. From uncovering your core values and embracing your unique strengths to mastering resilience and setting bold, authentic goals, this book equips you with everything you need to unlock your potential.

This isn't just another list of tips—it's a blueprint for creating a life that feels aligned with your true self. The book will inspire you to reframe your mindset, overcome self-doubt, and step forward with confidence. Through personal stories, empowering lessons, and practical exercises, *Unstoppable Woman* gives you the tools to shape your destiny and make empowered choices every single day.

Whether you're just starting on your journey or you're looking for the courage to take that next bold step, this book is a companion that will meet you where you are and help you rise to the next level. It's for women who know that they deserve more and are willing to do the work to claim it.

In this book, you'll find the encouragement to:

- Break through limiting beliefs that have held you back.
- Discover and live in alignment with your core values.
- Set meaningful goals that inspire action and fulfillment.
- Cultivate resilience, confidence, and self-love.
- Build a vision for your life that feels exciting, empowering, and uniquely yours.
- *Unstoppable Woman* is your invitation to take control of your life and create the success you deserve—on your own terms, and with full heart and soul. The time is now. You're ready

How to Read and Make the Most of this Book

Unstoppable Woman is a book you can approach on your own, or as a transformative experience to share with others. The beauty of this journey is that it can be tailored to fit whatever feels most empowering for you—whether you're diving deep in private reflection, discussing it with friends, or exploring it with a group of like-minded women.

Reading and Implementing Solo:

If you're reading this alone, consider it a personal journey toward a life you love. Treat each chapter as a gentle challenge to reflect, journal, and make small shifts in your daily life. To make the most of it, I recommend reading with a notebook by your side to jot down insights, aha moments, or any steps you feel inspired to try. Think of each chapter as an invitation to make changes that feel natural for you—step by step, at your own pace.

Studying with a Group or Team:

In a group or team setting, this book becomes an opportunity to share insights, support each other's growth, and create a shared vision of success. Consider reading a chapter together each week or month, then using the "Power Moves" to spark open discussions and exercises in a group session. Take turns sharing personal reflections, insights, and ways to apply the concepts in real life. The collective energy of a group can amplify your motivation and offer fresh perspectives.

Using This Book in a Training Program:

As part of a structured training or workshop, *Unstoppable Woman* can serve as a roadmap for growth, leadership, and empowerment. Each chapter can be adapted into a training module, with "Power Moves" acting as exercises to engage participants and spark reflection. Trainers and facilitators can create activities around these moves, including group discussions, action plans, and goal-setting exercises. Encourage participants to set individual and collective intentions to put these concepts into action, both in their personal and professional lives.

Whether you choose to explore these ideas on your own, with friends, or in a larger group, the steps in this book are meant to be actionable, adaptable, and, most of all, meaningful to you. Allow yourself to grow at a pace that feels right, and enjoy the journey—this book is yours to bring to life.

About the Author

Marsha Lynn Hudson, EdS

I'm Marsha Lynn Hudson, and I believe every woman has the potential to live a life she loves—full of purpose, passion, and success. I've always known that with the right mindset and consistent action, we can achieve what we set our minds to. That's why I'm so passionate about helping women unlock their full potential and create the life they dream of.

My journey started back in college when I first realized the power of self-development and empowerment. Since then, I've dedicated myself to helping women build a strong internal foundation, set meaningful goals, and take the right actions to bring those goals to life. What makes me unique in this work is my unwavering belief in others. I truly believe that with discipline and consistency, great things happen—and I'm here to help you see that for yourself.

My life and work are deeply rooted in my values. I trust in God as the creator and author of my life, and I live by biblical principles that guide my actions every day. Kindness, respect, and treating others the way I want to be treated are core to how I show up in the world. It's these principles that drive my desire to see women step into their full potential and live a life of purpose.

For 27 years, I had the privilege of serving as a Professor of Writing. Teaching in the classroom was something I truly loved, and I was fortunate enough to travel and speak at conferences, igniting change and inspiring those around me. Along with being a professor, I'm also a photographer, writer, author, and speaker. I've learned that the power of creativity, storytelling, and connection can spark real transformation, and I've built my career around sharing those gifts with others.

I know that change can be overwhelming, which is why I keep things simple and actionable. My goal is to inspire you to take the steps necessary for transformation—whether it's in your mindset, goals, or actions. What excites me most about the work I do is seeing people's lives transformed. I truly believe that we all have a good plan for our lives, and success is not just about us—it's about helping others succeed too.

When I'm not coaching, speaking, or training, you can often find me at a local coffee house with a book in one hand and a coffee in the other, enjoying the simple pleasures of life. I am married to my best friend and biggest supporter, Malcom Hudson. Together, we share a life full of love, respect, purpose, and peace. We enjoy short get a ways, listening to music and just hanging out.

As you read my book, I hope you'll find the clarity and motivation to create the life you desire. I'm here to cheer you on every step of the way, knowing that with a little belief and action, you can have everything you want.

To your abundant success,

Marsha

Table of Content

Part 1-

Unstoppable Woman

Create a Life You Love

Power Move 1:
Unstoppable Mindset: Cultivating a Powerful Attitude for Success

This power move will cultivate a resilient mindset that empowers you to see obstacles as stepping stones, shifting your perspective to focus on growth and opportunity. Embracing this mindset will fuel your confidence, enabling you to take on challenges with strength and optimism.

Every challenge you face is an opportunity to grow. Embracing an unstoppable mindset can turn setbacks into stepping stones. Imagine transforming obstacles into the very fuel that propels you toward success.

"The only limit to our realization of tomorrow is our doubts of today." – Eleanor Roosevelt

An unstoppable mindset is essential for achieving long-term success. It involves maintaining a positive outlook and using setbacks as learning opportunities. By focusing on solutions rather than problems, you can shift your perspective and remain motivated even in tough times.

Reframing negative thoughts into constructive ones is a powerful technique. When faced with challenges, ask yourself what you can learn and how you can use this experience to grow. This shift in mindset will help you overcome obstacles and move forward with renewed determination.

Daily gratitude is a practice that strengthens your resilience. By regularly acknowledging the things you're thankful for, you build a positive outlook that helps you navigate difficulties more effectively. Gratitude fosters a mindset that sees opportunities even in adversity.

Setting achievable goals provides direction and motivation. Break down your larger objectives into smaller, manageable steps to create a clear path forward. Achieving these smaller milestones will boost your confidence and keep you focused on your long-term vision.

Another key aspect of an unstoppable mindset is developing a growth-oriented perspective. When you start to see every experience—whether positive or challenging—as an opportunity for learning, you transform how you approach life itself. This attitude empowers you to adapt to change with ease and embrace life's unknowns with curiosity and strength.

Building a supportive network is essential. Surround yourself with people who uplift and inspire you. This network can offer encouragement and advice when you face challenges, providing a boost of motivation and perspective. Together, you become unstoppable, each person adding strength to the other.

An Unstoppable Woman's Story:

A woman faced a major career setback when she was passed over for a promotion she had worked hard for. Instead of letting it defeat her, she chose to view it as a learning opportunity. She took this time to upskill, seek feedback, and set new career goals. Her positive attitude and determination paid off when she not only achieved her career goals but surpassed them, eventually landing a role she had always dreamed of. Her story is a reminder that every obstacle can be a stepping stone if we choose to see it that way.

3-Step Process:

- **Reframe Challenges:** Practice seeing obstacles as opportunities to learn and grow.
- **Set Small Goals:** Break larger ambitions into manageable steps that keep you motivated.
- **Build Your Network:** Connect with others who support and uplift you on your journey.

Unstoppable Woman – Take Action – Your Turn:

Identify three recent challenges you've faced. For each, write down one positive outcome or lesson learned. Use these lessons to create a brief plan for handling similar challenges in the future.

Write it Down:

Think of a time when your mindset helped you overcome a challenge. How did your attitude impact the outcome?

Key Takeaways:

- An unstoppable mindset turns challenges into growth opportunities.
- Reframe negative thoughts and focus on solutions.
- Practice daily gratitude and set clear goals.
- Build a supportive network for encouragement and advice.

Summary:

Cultivating an unstoppable mindset helps turn challenges into opportunities for success. By reframing negative thoughts, practicing gratitude, and setting achievable goals, you lay a strong foundation for overcoming obstacles. Embrace every challenge as a chance to grow and enhance your mindset, knowing your attitude influences your success.

The Unstoppable Woman's Affirmation- Say It Out Loud

"I embrace every challenge as an opportunity to grow and strengthen my resolve. I believe in my ability to overcome setbacks and transform obstacles into stepping stones. My mindset is powerful, and I choose resilience, positivity, and gratitude every day. I am unstoppable, and my journey is fueled by my inner strength and determination."

My Story

When I think about mindset, I'm reminded of a time in my life when I felt completely stuck. Everything felt uphill, like each day was a new obstacle course of self-doubt, criticism, and fear. I remember wanting to step out, try something bold, but the voice in my head was loud and relentless.

"Who are you kidding? Do you really think you're capable of this?" It took time, patience, and a lot of learning, but I came to realize that mindset is everything. It's the lens through which we see our lives and measure our worth. Once I started shifting that lens and practicing gratitude, resilience, and a growth attitude, doors opened, and I started seeing my potential.

Be "You" Unstoppable Woman

Embracing an unstoppable mindset begins with fully accepting who you are—flaws, strengths, dreams, and all. No one can think, create, or be exactly like you. This journey is about recognizing that your uniqueness is what makes you powerful. Lean into your individual strengths, and use them to forge a path that aligns with your vision.

How Can I Incorporate this Power Move into My Life?

Start each day by listing one thing you're grateful for and one challenge you're ready to tackle, setting the tone for a growth-oriented mindset.

Words from Marsha:

"Your mindset is your most powerful tool. Embrace every challenge as a chance to grow stronger and keep pushing forward. Believe in your potential, and there's no limit to what you can achieve."

Power Move 2
Unstoppable Goals: Creating a Focused Path to Success

This power move will help you set clear, meaningful goals that align with your true desires and values. By creating a focused vision, you'll be able to design a path to success that feels purposeful and achievable, setting you up for a journey of consistent progress.

Setting unstoppable goals is about more than just dreaming big – it's about defining a path that aligns with who you are and where you truly want to go. When your goals are driven by your personal values, they fuel your passion and keep you moving forward with purpose, even when obstacles arise. Unstoppable goals give your life direction and turn your aspirations into reality.

"Setting goals is the first step in turning the invisible into the visible." – Tony Robbins

To create a focused path to success, you need clear, actionable, and meaningful goals. These goals serve as the roadmap that guides you toward your vision and help you stay aligned with your purpose. When you set goals that matter to you personally, you are more likely to stay committed, motivated, and excited about the journey. Unstoppable goals make it possible to turn even the loftiest dreams into achievable steps.

Unstoppable goals begin with clarity. You need a clear understanding of what you want to accomplish and why it matters to you. Define what success looks like for you – not just in terms of tangible achievements but also in how it aligns with your values and brings fulfillment to your life. This clarity helps you avoid setting goals based on others' expectations and keeps you focused on what truly matters to you.

Life will bring changes, and goals may need to be adapted along the way. Embrace adjustments as part of the journey instead of feeling like a setback. Staying flexible means, you can continue moving forward, even if the path changes. Flexibility allows you to adapt without losing sight of your ultimate vision.

Accountability is also essential in reaching unstoppable goals. Sharing your goals with a friend, joining a support group, or setting up regular check-ins can help you stay focused and driven. When you have people who encourage and support your journey, you'll be more likely to overcome challenges and persevere. Their belief in you becomes a source of motivation during difficult times, reminding you that you're not alone in pursuing your dreams.

Embrace the idea that each goal achieved is a building block in your journey. When you reach a milestone, celebrate it, but remember that each accomplishment is part of a greater vision. Setting unstoppable goals is about ongoing growth, with each success guiding you closer to a life that reflects who you truly are and what you are capable of achieving.

An Unstoppable Woman's Story:

A woman set a goal to launch her own business, something she had dreamed of for years. With a busy career and family responsibilities, she felt uncertain if she could make it happen. Instead of letting doubt hold her back, she began by breaking her goal into small steps: researching her industry, finding mentors, and setting up a timeline. As she tackled each step, she gained momentum and confidence. Despite setbacks, she remained flexible, adapting her approach as needed. Eventually, she launched her business successfully, and her commitment to her goals transformed her dream into reality. Her journey reminds us that when we break down goals and stay adaptable, we can accomplish even our biggest aspirations.

3-Step Process:

- **Get Clear on Your "Why":** Make sure your goals align with your values and what truly matters to you.
- **Break It Down:** Divide big goals into small, manageable steps to create a clear path forward.
- **Build Accountability:** Surround yourself with people who encourage and support your journey.

Unstoppable Woman – Take Action – Your Turn:

Write down three specific goals that align with your values and long-term vision. Next to each goal, list the smaller steps you can take to start making progress toward them. For each step, note a target date to keep yourself accountable and motivated.

Write t Down:

- **Reflect on your "why":** What personal values or aspirations are driving this goal? Why is it important to you?
- **Break it into steps:** How can you break this goal into smaller, manageable steps to track progress?
- **Plan for obstacles:** What challenges might you face, and how can you prepare to overcome them?

Key Takeaways:

- Align your goals with personal values for meaningful progress.
- Break large goals into smaller steps to create steady, achievable progress.
- Use flexibility to adapt when needed and keep moving forward.
- Accountability with friends, mentors, or support groups strengthens commitment.

Summary:

Setting unstoppable goals provides a focused path to success. By aligning goals with your values, breaking them into manageable steps, and staying flexible, you can make steady progress toward any aspiration. Surround yourself with encouragement and remember that every step forward counts. Together, these strategies make it possible to turn your dreams into a focused, unstoppable journey.

The Unstoppable Woman's Affirmation- Say It Out Loud

"I set clear, meaningful goals that align with my true values and vision. Every goal I pursue brings me closer to the life I desire. I am focused, purposeful, and committed to my journey. My actions are intentional, and I trust in my ability to achieve each milestone. I am unstoppable, creating a future that reflects my dreams and aspirations."

My Story

Setting goals was something I used to do casually, like jotting down a few ideas here and there, but I wasn't actually putting in the work to create a path for my dreams. It wasn't until I faced a major setback that I realized I needed to get intentional about my goals, break them down, and give them my full attention.

I started small, setting realistic goals that I knew I could tackle. Each milestone gave me a sense of accomplishment, and with time, I learned to trust the process. The power of goal-setting transformed my life and taught me that there is incredible strength in defining your path, however big or small.

Words from Marsha:

"Each goal you set is a declaration of your commitment to your dreams. Don't be afraid to aim high, stay flexible, and surround yourself with people who cheer you on. With each step, you're not just reaching goals – you're creating a life that's truly yours.

How Can I Incorporate this Power Move into My Life?

Write down one small, achievable goal each morning—something you can check off by day's end—to keep your momentum strong and focused.

Be "You" – Unstoppable Woman

"The courage to set meaningful goals is the courage to define your own path. Follow what matters to you, and you'll find that nothing is out of reach."

Power Move 3
Unstoppable Confidence: Building Authentic Self-Assurance to Step Boldly into Your Potential

This power move will build a foundation of unshakeable self-confidence, allowing you to embrace new opportunities and own your place in the world. With a sense of genuine self-worth, you'll step forward boldly and assertively, ready to conquer anything that comes your way.

Confidence is the bridge between dreams and reality. When you believe in yourself, you unlock the power to face new challenges, seize opportunities, and show up authentically in every setting. Confidence is not about being fearless; it's about feeling the fear and moving forward anyway. Embracing self-assurance allows you to pursue your aspirations with conviction and lets you own your space unapologetically.

"With confidence, you have won before you have started."
– Marcus Garvey

An unstoppable confidence begins with self-acceptance. When you fully accept who you are, flaws and all, you develop a sense of security that frees you from seeking external validation. This inner confidence allows you to be genuine and grounded, knowing that you bring something valuable to the table. As you let go of the need for approval, you'll find that your energy and focus shift toward what truly matters to you.

To build this confidence, it's crucial to recognize your unique strengths. Take time to acknowledge what you bring to the world, whether it's your creativity, compassion, or problem-solving skills. By focusing on what you're naturally good at, you create a foundation of self-trust. Every time you lean into these strengths, you reinforce your confidence, making it easier to navigate challenges and embrace new roles.

Self-confidence also involves learning to quiet your inner critic. That voice in your head may tell you that you're not enough, that others are better, or that success is out of reach. Instead of allowing it to undermine you, recognize that it's simply a sign of self-doubt. Challenge these thoughts by reminding yourself of past achievements and the qualities that make you unique. This practice builds resilience against negative self-talk and empowers you to step out of your comfort zone.

Embracing vulnerability is another powerful component of confidence. Allowing yourself to be open and authentic, even when it feels uncomfortable, fosters genuine connections with others. When you show up as you are, people see your courage and authenticity, which builds mutual respect and trust. In turn, this strengthens your confidence and reinforces the belief that you're worthy of being seen and valued for who you are.

An Unstoppable Woman's Story

A woman once found herself in a new role that felt far beyond her abilities. She doubted herself daily, feeling as if she wasn't equipped to handle the responsibilities. Yet, instead of letting the self-doubt paralyze her, she chose to approach each day as a learning experience. She focused on one task at a time, seeking help when needed and reminding herself of her previous accomplishments. Over time, her confidence grew as she realized she could master the role. This confidence eventually led her to excel and even train others for similar positions, transforming her once uncertain beginning into a source of personal and professional strength.

3-Step Process:

- **Shift Your Focus** – Replace self-doubt with empowering thoughts.
- **Celebrate Small Wins** – Acknowledge your progress, no matter how small.
- **Embody Confidence** – Choose to act with confidence, even in discomfort.

Unstoppable Woman – Take Action – Your Turn:

- **Reflect:** Think about a time you felt confident. What was different? How did it impact your results?
- **Write it down:** List 3 actions to take today to boost your confidence.
- **Commit:** Choose one daily habit to practice for building lasting confidence.

Write it Down

- Reflect on a time when you felt confident and capable. What were the circumstances, and how did that confidence impact the outcome?
- Think about an area in your life where you'd like to build more confidence. What small actions can you start taking today to strengthen your self-assurance?

- List three unique strengths or qualities you possess. How can you use these strengths to support your goals and boost your confidence?

Key Takeaways

- Confidence is built through self-acceptance and embracing your strengths.
- Challenge your inner critic and replace negative thoughts with empowering beliefs.
- Vulnerability and authenticity foster genuine connections and boost self-assurance.
- Visualization is a tool to mentally prepare for confidence in action.
- Confidence is a journey, strengthened through consistent, courageous steps

Summary

Developing unstoppable confidence empowers you to take bold steps in the direction of your dreams. By acknowledging your strengths, silencing self-doubt, and embracing authenticity, you create a solid foundation for self-assurance. Confidence grows through action, small steps that lead to big transformations over time. Embrace each day as an opportunity to show up fully and build the self-trust that will guide you to success.

Unstoppable Woman's Affirmation- Say It Out Loud

"I am worthy of every opportunity that comes my way. I embrace my unique strengths and step confidently into my potential. My self-belief grows with each action I take. I trust in my abilities, knowing that confidence is built through courage and self-acceptance. I am unstoppable, empowered, and ready to shine."

My Story

Confidence didn't come naturally to me. I was someone who often held back, who questioned my worth and let opportunities pass me by because I didn't feel "good enough." But there came a point where I realized that staying in my shell was keeping me from the life I truly wanted. So, I took a deep breath and began stepping out—sometimes clumsily, often with fear, but always moving forward.

Each time I pushed past my comfort zone, I grew a little stronger, a little more assured. This chapter is about that same journey for you, about realizing that confidence is something you build from within, one step at a time. My hope is to help you see that you can walk into any room, any opportunity, and own it.

Words from Marsha

"Confidence isn't about always having the answers or never feeling doubt. It's about trusting yourself enough to keep moving forward, even when the path isn't clear. Confidence is built in the moments when you decide to show up as you are, flaws and all.

How Can I Incorporate this Power Move into My Life?

Practice positive self-talk by telling yourself, "I am capable," whenever you feel doubt. Let this affirmation become a daily habit.

Be "You" Unstoppable Woman

"Confidence is your power, and the world needs what only you can bring. When you embrace who you are unapologetically, you inspire others to do the same. Being unstoppable doesn't mean you're perfect—it means you're real, resilient, and ready to rise above any challenge.

Power Move 4
Unstoppable Action: Embracing the Courage to Take Decisive Steps Toward Your Goals

This power move will inspire you to take focused, consistent action toward your goals. You'll find the courage to push past hesitation and procrastination, making steady progress and building momentum with every step forward.

Action is the heartbeat of success. Without action, even the best plans and intentions remain dreams. An unstoppable woman knows that it's not just about thinking big—it's about doing big. It's about having the courage to take that first step, even when the path ahead feels uncertain. Taking action moves you from dreaming about success to living it.

"Action is the foundational key to all success." — Pablo Picasso

The courage to take action doesn't always mean charging ahead with unwavering confidence. Often, it means moving forward with uncertainty and fear, but doing it anyway. It means showing up even when you feel unprepared or unsure. Unstoppable women know that waiting for the "perfect moment" can lead to endless hesitation. Instead, they take action in the now—because progress, no matter how small, is still progress.

One powerful tool in embracing action is breaking big tasks into smaller, manageable steps. When a goal feels overwhelming, it can be easy to procrastinate. But by breaking it down into bite-sized pieces, you transform the impossible into the possible. Each small step taken is a victory, and it builds momentum toward the larger goal. With each action, the process becomes less intimidating and more achievable.

Overcoming fear is an integral part of taking action. Fear is a natural response, but it doesn't have to control you. Instead of letting fear paralyze you, use it as fuel. The most successful people are often the ones who've learned to feel the fear and do it anyway. Unstoppable women don't allow fear to stop them—they use it to push them forward, knowing that the greatest rewards lie just beyond the discomfort.

Accountability is another key to taking consistent action. When you make your goals public or share them with others, you create a system of accountability that helps you stay on track. Whether it's a mentor, a coach, or a friend, having someone to check in with can keep you motivated and prevent you from slipping back into procrastination

The key to unstoppable action is consistency. Even on days when motivation is low or doubt creeps in, continue taking steps forward. It's the consistency in your actions that compounds over time and creates lasting change. Unstoppable women know that even the smallest consistent effort eventually leads to monumental transformation.

An Unstoppable Woman's Story

A woman once dreamed of starting her own business, but every time she thought about taking the leap, fear and doubt would hold her back. She told herself that she needed more research, more time, more resources. But one day, she decided to stop waiting for the "perfect moment." She took a small step—she registered her business name and set up a basic website. Then, she reached out to one potential client. Every day, she took one more small action: a phone call, an email, a social media post. Slowly but surely, her business began to grow. She learned that taking action, even in small doses, was the key to creating the life she had always wanted. Today, her business is thriving, and she's proud of herself for taking that first step, no matter how small it seemed at the time.

3-Step Process:

- **Break It Down** – Divide big goals into smaller, manageable steps.
- **Create a Routine** – Set daily habits that keep you moving forward.
- **Push Through Resistance** – Embrace discomfort and keep moving anyway.

Unstoppable Woman – Take Action – Your Turn:

- **Reflect:** What's one goal you've been avoiding? Break it down into 3 smaller steps.
- **Take Action:** Focus on one step and take action today, even if it's just for 10 minutes.
- **Accountability:** Share your goal with someone who can help keep you accountable.

Write it Down

- Reflect on a goal you've been putting off. What's one small action you can take today to move it forward?
- Think about a time when you overcame fear to take action. What did you learn from that experience, and how did it push you forward?
- Identify one area of your life where you tend to procrastinate. What small, simple step can you take today to begin making progress?

Key Takeaways

- Taking action is essential for turning dreams into reality.
- Break big goals into smaller, manageable tasks to avoid feeling overwhelmed.
- Use fear as motivation and move forward even when uncertainty is present.
- Accountability partners help you stay on track and keep you motivated.
- Consistency is the key to achieving big results over time

Summary

Unstoppable action is the bridge between your goals and their realization. It's about taking consistent, deliberate steps, even when fear or doubt try to hold you back. Every small action counts, and with each step forward, momentum builds. Remember, waiting for the "perfect moment" only delays progress. Instead, start now, and keep going—because action is the foundation of success.

Unstoppable Woman's Affirmation- Say It Out Loud

"I take decisive action toward my goals every day. I move forward with courage, even when I feel fear, knowing that progress is built one step at a time. I trust in my ability to take the next step, and I believe that every action, no matter how small, brings me closer to my dreams. I am unstoppable, and my actions reflect my commitment to success."

My Story

There was a time in my life when I was full of ideas but not actions. I'd dream and plan, envision a future full of possibilities, but when it came to moving forward, I would stall. The fear of failure and the weight of procrastination held me back. One day, I realized that nothing was going to happen unless I took that first step, however imperfect. So, I did. That small act of starting—of getting up and actually taking action—was a game-changer. I learned that action creates momentum and that consistency, no matter how small, leads to big results over time

Words from Marsha

"Action is the key to transformation. You can have the best ideas, the most beautiful goals, and the greatest plans—but without action, they remain just that—ideas. It's the steps you take each day, even the smallest ones, that add up and create the change you desire. Don't wait for the perfect time. Start now. The future belongs to those who take consistent action today."

Be "You" Unstoppable Woman

Taking action means showing up authentically in everything you do. Don't wait for the perfect moment or the perfect version of yourself to begin; start right now, with who you are and where you are. Trust that your unique qualities, experiences, and perspective are exactly what's needed to make a difference.

How Can I Incorporate this Power Move into My Life?

Take one proactive step toward a goal daily, no matter how small. Small actions create the momentum that leads to big change.

Power Move 5
Unstoppable Resilience: Bouncing Back Stronger From Setbacks

This power move will equip you with the strength to handle setbacks and challenges with grace. You'll learn to bounce back from difficulties with renewed energy, using every experience as fuel to propel yourself closer to your dreams.

Resilience is the ability to bounce back from life's challenges and setbacks. It's not about avoiding difficulties—because we all face them. It's about how we respond to them. When you're an unstoppable woman, resilience becomes your superpower. It's the inner strength that helps you keep going, even when life feels like it's throwing everything at you. Instead of giving up, you keep moving forward, knowing that every challenge is an opportunity to grow.

"It's not how far you fall, but how high you bounce that counts." — Zig Ziglar

Resilience isn't something that comes naturally to everyone, but it's something you can build. It starts with shifting your mindset. When life throws you a curveball, it's easy to spiral into frustration, anger, or self-doubt. But resilient women know that setbacks are temporary. They don't allow failure to define them. Instead, they view it as part of the journey and as an essential lesson for future success.

One of the keys to resilience is maintaining a positive perspective. When things go wrong, it's easy to get stuck in a negative mindset. But a resilient woman knows that adversity is often a hidden blessing. Challenges force you to get creative, problem-solve, and adapt. When you see setbacks as learning experiences rather than roadblocks, it empowers you to move forward with strength and determination.

Building emotional strength is another aspect of resilience. Life is filled with ups and downs, but how you manage your emotions makes all the difference. Resilient women don't ignore their feelings, but they don't let them control their actions either. They know how to process their emotions, learn from them, and keep going. Emotional strength comes from acknowledging the pain, disappointment, or fear, but choosing to rise above it instead of staying stuck.

In times of adversity, it's also important to lean on your support system. An unstoppable woman doesn't have to face every challenge alone. Surrounding yourself with people who believe in you and support your goals is crucial. Whether it's friends, family, or a mentor, having a solid support system can offer encouragement, guidance, and perspective when you need it most.

Resilience also means being adaptable. Life rarely goes according to plan, and the ability to pivot when things don't go as expected is essential. Unstoppable women are flexible in their approach and open to change. Resilience is about perseverance. It's about not giving up when it's hard.. Unstoppable women have the grit to keep going even when the road gets tough.

An Unstoppable Woman's Story

A woman had worked tirelessly to build her dream business, only to face a major financial setback that almost put her out of business. The stress and fear weighed heavily on her, and she questioned if she should just give up. But she didn't. She reached out to her mentors, reassessed her strategy, and found new ways to make her business thrive. She focused on her strengths, adjusted her approach, and started small again. With each small step forward, she gained confidence. Her business didn't just recover—it came back stronger than before. The experience taught her that resilience isn't just about bouncing back; it's about becoming better, wiser, and more determined after every setback.

3-Step Process:

- **Reframe Setbacks** – View challenges as opportunities to learn.
- **Build a Support System** – Surround yourself with people who lift you up.
- **Practice Patience** – Trust that growth takes time and setbacks don't define you.

Unstoppable Woman – Take Action – Your Turn:

- **Reflect:** Recall a recent setback. How did you respond? What did you learn?
- **Take Action:** Identify one small step today to bounce back from a challenge.

Write it Down

- Think about a time when you faced a difficult challenge. What did you learn from it that helped you grow stronger?

- How do you typically respond when things don't go as planned? What could you do differently to bounce back more effectively next time?
- Identify one current setback in your life. What is one small action you can take today to begin turning it around?

Key Takeaways

- Resilience is the ability to recover from setbacks and continue moving forward.
- A positive perspective allows you to view challenges as opportunities for growth.
- Emotional strength helps you navigate tough times without letting your feelings dictate your actions.
- Surround yourself with a supportive network to help you bounce back when life gets tough.
- Adaptability is key—be willing to pivot when plans fall through.
- Perseverance is the secret to long-term success; never give up, no matter the setbacks.

Summary

Resilience isn't about avoiding obstacles; it's about how you handle them. When you embrace setbacks as part of the process, you develop the strength to keep going. By maintaining a positive perspective, building emotional strength, and being adaptable, you'll not only bounce back stronger, but you'll also grow into a more unstoppable version of yourself. Keep moving forward, and remember, setbacks are just stepping stones on your journey to success.

Unstoppable Woman's Affirmation- Say It Out Loud

"I am resilient. I embrace challenges and use them as opportunities to grow. When life gets tough, I bounce back stronger, wiser, and more determined. I trust in my ability to overcome any obstacle and know that every setback is simply a lesson in disguise. I am unstoppable, and I rise above all challenges with grace and confidence."

My Story

Life threw some tough challenges my way, ones I never expected and certainly didn't feel ready to handle. At one point, I thought I couldn't keep going, that maybe I'd reached my limit. But then I remembered the strength I'd seen in others who had walked difficult paths and come through stronger. I decided that no matter how many times I was knocked down, I'd get back up—bruised, maybe, but still standing. Resilience became my lifeline. Every challenge became fuel, every setback a lesson.

Words from Marsha

"Resilience is not about avoiding failure; it's about how you respond when failure knocks at your door. You have the power to rise up, learn from your mistakes, and become even stronger. Life will test you, but you get to decide how you respond. Choose to bounce back, learn from your experiences, and keep moving forward—because your ability to bounce back is what will set you apart."

How Can I Incorporate this Power Move into My Life?

When something doesn't go as planned, pause and ask, "What can I learn from this?" This keeps you focused on growth, not setbacks.

Be "You" Unstoppable Woman

"Every challenge you face is shaping you into the woman you were meant to be. Don't shy away from adversity—embrace it. You have everything you need within you to rise above anything that comes your way. Be unapologetically YOU, with all your strength, your wisdom, and your resilience. The world needs your unique power. Stand tall, face your challenges head-on, and show the world just how unstoppable you truly are.

Power Move 6
Unstoppable Self-Care: Nourishing Your Mind, Body, and Spirit

This power move will remind you to prioritize your well-being, nurturing your body, mind, and spirit. By committing to self-care, you'll maintain the energy and balance needed to pursue your goals while staying grounded, healthy, and empowered on your journey.

Self-care isn't a luxury; it's a necessity. To show up as your best self in the world, you must first take care of yourself. We often get so caught up in helping others, working on our businesses, or pursuing our dreams that we forget about the most important thing—our own well-being. But remember this: You can't pour from an empty cup. When you nourish your mind, body, and spirit, you have the energy and vitality to give your best to the people and projects you care about. Self-care is the fuel that powers your unstoppable journey.

"Self-care is not a waste of time; self-care makes your use of time more sustainable." – Jackie Viramontez

Self-care is about more than just pampering yourself with spa days or bubble baths (though those are nice too!). It's about creating habits that nurture your physical, emotional, and mental well-being. It's about setting boundaries so you don't burn out. It's about saying no when necessary and prioritizing your health, peace, and happiness. When you prioritize yourself, you are telling the universe that you value your own needs, and that self-respect reflects in everything you do.

Taking care of your body is a fundamental part of self-care. Your body is your vehicle for moving through the world, and it deserves to be treated with kindness. This means eating nutritious foods, exercising regularly, getting enough sleep, and staying hydrated. It's easy to neglect your physical health when life gets busy, but even small changes can make a big difference. Taking just a few minutes each day to stretch, walk, or meditate will leave you feeling more energized and ready to take on the world.

Self-care also involves investing in your personal growth. Take time for activities that bring you joy, inspire creativity, or help you expand your knowledge. Read books that uplift you, listen to podcasts that motivate you, or take a class that enhances your skills. When you continue to grow and evolve, you become a more confident, capable, and unstoppable woman.

Remember, self-care is not selfish—it's an investment in your future. By taking time to nurture yourself, you become more resilient, more effective, and more empowered to live the life you desire. Self-care is the foundation for everything you want to achieve. If you don't take care of yourself, you won't have the energy or focus to take care of your dreams, your family, or your business. You deserve to feel your best, so you can give your best.

An Unstoppable Woman's Story

A woman worked tirelessly on her career and business, always putting others first. But over time, she started feeling drained, overwhelmed, and burnt out. Her energy was low, and she was losing her passion for the work she loved. One day, she realized she was running on empty—and that something had to change. She decided to make self-care a priority, starting with small daily habits like meditating each morning, getting regular exercise, and setting clear boundaries at work. Slowly but surely, she began to feel recharged, refocused, and reconnected to her purpose. With renewed energy, she approached her work and her life with a newfound sense of clarity and confidence. Prioritizing her well-being helped her step back into her power, and she found herself more successful than ever.

3-Step Process:

- **Prioritize Yourself** – Schedule time each day just for you.
- **Nourish Your Mind and Body** – Feed your mind with positivity and your body with health.
- **Set Boundaries** – Protect your time and energy to give your best.

Unstoppable Woman – Take Action – Your Turn:

- **Reflect:** When was the last time you took care of yourself? What did you do?
- **Take Action:** Choose one act of self-care to do today, whether it's taking a walk or reading.
- **Plan:** Block out 30 minutes this week for something nourishing for your mind and body.

Write it Down

- Think about how you currently take care of yourself—physically, mentally, and emotionally. What areas need more attention?

- What are some self-care activities that you can incorporate into your daily routine to feel more balanced and energized?
- How can you set boundaries in your life to protect your time, energy, and peace of mind?

Key Takeaways

- Self-care is essential for maintaining balance, focus, and energy.
- Physical health is the foundation of self-care—prioritize exercise, nutrition, and rest.
- Mental and emotional health require nurturing through mindfulness, boundaries, and emotional expression.
- Investing in personal growth and creative activities fuels your unstoppable potential.
- Self-care is an investment in your future—it helps you show up as the best version of yourself.

Summary

Taking care of yourself isn't a luxury; it's a necessity for your success. By nurturing your mind, body, and spirit, you create a solid foundation for living a fulfilling and unstoppable life. Self-care gives you the energy, clarity, and confidence to pursue your goals, overcome challenges, and show up in the world with power. You are worthy of the time and attention it takes to care for yourself—because when you feel your best, you are unstoppable.

Unstoppable Woman's Affirmation- Say It Out Loud

"I am worthy of love, care, and attention. I nourish my body, mind, and spirit with kindness, balance, and peace. I prioritize my well-being, knowing that by taking care of myself, I am more capable of achieving my dreams and supporting others. I am strong, I am resilient, and I am unstoppable."

My Story

For years, I saw self-care as a luxury, something I'd "get around to" once everything else was taken care of. But I learned the hard way that neglecting myself was a one-way ticket to burnout. Eventually, I had to stop and ask myself, "How can I pour into others if I'm running on empty?" I started making time for myself—mindfully and unapologetically.

From taking breaks to focusing on what nourishes my body and soul, self-care became the foundation of everything I did. This chapter is about that journey, about realizing that caring for ourselves is essential, not optional. I hope it helps you see that your well-being isn't selfish; it's the fuel that will carry you through every challenge and victory along your path.

Words from Marsha

"Self-care is the bedrock of everything you want to achieve. When you make time for yourself, you're not only honoring your body and mind, but you're also giving yourself the strength to rise above life's challenges. Remember, you can't pour from an empty cup. Fill yourself up, so you can show up fully for the world."

How Can I Incorporate this Power Move into My Life?

Set aside five minutes each day for yourself—whether it's deep breathing, stretching, or savoring a quiet moment—because even a few minutes can recharge your spirit.

Be "You" Unstoppable Woman

"The world needs you at your best—mentally, physically, and emotionally. By taking care of yourself, you are honoring your purpose and your potential. Don't wait for someone else to take care of you—be the one to nurture your soul, your body, and your dreams. You are your greatest asset, and when you invest in yourself, you'll be unstoppable."

Part 2-
Unstoppable Woman Achieve the Success You Deserve

Power Move 7
Unstoppable Vision: Creating Your Path to Extraordinary Success

This power move will: Transform how you view your future by helping you create a crystal-clear picture of your ideal life, giving you both direction and motivation to make that vision reality.

Your vision is your North Star—it guides every decision, action, and step you take on your journey to success. Without a clear vision, you're like a ship without a destination, drifting wherever the winds take you. But when you have a compelling vision for your life and career, you become unstoppable. Your vision gives you purpose, direction, and the motivation to push through any obstacles that stand in your way.

"Vision is not just a picture of what could be; it is an appeal to our better selves, a call to become something more." — Rosabeth Moss Kanter

Creating a vision isn't just about dreaming big—it's about getting crystal clear on what you truly want and why you want it. Your vision should excite you, challenge you, and pull you forward into your greatest potential. It should align with your values, tap into your passions, and reflect the impact you want to make in the world. When your vision resonates deeply with who you are and what matters most to you, it becomes a powerful force that drives you toward extraordinary achievement.

Your vision should encompass all areas of your life—not just your career or business goals. Consider what you want in your relationships, health, personal growth, and contribution to others. A truly unstoppable vision creates harmony between different aspects of your life, ensuring that success in one area doesn't come at the expense of another. When your vision is holistic, you can pursue your goals with confidence, knowing that you're creating a life that feels fulfilling on all levels.

Visualization is a powerful tool for bringing your vision to life. Take time regularly to see yourself living your vision—feel the emotions, imagine the details, and experience the satisfaction of achieving what you've set out to do. This practice helps program your mind for success and keeps you focused on your desired outcomes. The more vividly you can imagine your vision, the more real and achievable it becomes.

Implementation is where vision becomes reality. Break down your big vision into actionable steps and create a strategic plan for moving forward. Set both short-term and long-term goals that align with your vision, and track your progress regularly. Remember that every small step you take brings you closer to your vision, and celebrating these milestones helps maintain momentum and motivation.

Your vision should inspire not just you, but others as well. When you can clearly communicate your vision, you attract like-minded people, resources, and opportunities that help bring it to life.

An Unstoppable Woman's Story

Samantha had always worked in corporate finance but felt a deeper calling to make a difference in women's lives. Through careful reflection and visualization, she developed a clear vision of creating a financial education platform specifically designed for women entrepreneurs. While maintaining her day job, she began taking steps toward her vision—studying online education, building a network of potential collaborators, and creating initial content. Within two years, her vision evolved into a thriving business that has helped thousands of women achieve financial independence. Her clear vision gave her the courage to transition from her corporate role and the persistence to overcome numerous challenges along the way.

Write it Down

1. What does your ideal life look like in 3-5 years across all areas: career, relationships, health, and personal growth?
2. What impact do you want to make in the world, and how does your vision align with this purpose?
3. What specific steps can you take in the next 90 days to move closer to your vision?

Key Takeaways

- A clear vision provides direction and purpose for all your actions and decisions
- Your vision should be comprehensive, covering all aspects of your life
- Regular visualization helps program your mind for success

- Breaking down your vision into actionable steps makes it achievable
- Sharing your vision attracts support and resources to help make it reality

My story

> I remember when: I sat down one Sunday afternoon with a blank journal, feeling lost about my next career move. Instead of making lists, I closed my eyes and really let myself imagine my ideal future 1-2 years out — the life I was living, what impact I was making, and how I felt about the life I was creating for myself each day.

How Can I Incorporate This Power Move Into My Life?

Pick a quiet spot at home and spend 10 minutes writing down exactly what you want your life to look like in 3 years - from your career to your relationships to where you live. Be specific. Read this vision every Monday morning while you drink your coffee or tea.

Summary

Your vision is the foundation of your unstoppable journey. By creating a clear, compelling vision that aligns with your values and excites your spirit, you set yourself up for extraordinary success. Remember that your vision is not just about what you want to achieve—it's about who you want to become and the impact you want to make. When you combine a powerful vision with strategic action, you become truly unstoppable.

Unstoppable Woman's Affirmation- Say It Out Loud

"I have a clear and compelling vision for my life that inspires and motivates me. I take bold action toward my vision every day, knowing that each step brings me closer to my dreams. My vision serves as my compass, guiding me toward extraordinary achievement and meaningful impact. I am focused, determined, and unstoppable in pursuing my vision."

Words from Marsha

"Your vision is your permission slip to dream bigger than you ever thought possible. Don't let anyone dim your vision or tell you it's too ambitious. The world needs women who dare to imagine extraordinary possibilities and have the courage to pursue them. Your vision is your gift to the world—honor it, nurture it, and watch it transform into reality."

3-Step Process:

- **Define Your Vision** – Clarify what you truly want for your future.
- **Visualize It Daily** – Imagine living your vision with all the emotions that come with it.
- **Create a Vision Board** – Use images and words to bring your vision to life visually.

Unstoppable Woman – Take Action – Your Turn:

- **Reflect:** What is your ultimate vision? How does it make you feel?
- **Take Action:** Create a vision board or write a description of your future vision.

- **Commit:** Set a time each day to visualize yourself living out that vision.

Be "You" Unstoppable Woman

"Your vision is uniquely yours—it reflects your values, your passions, and your highest potential. Don't be afraid to think big and push beyond conventional boundaries. When you align your actions with a clear and compelling vision, you become a force of nature. Trust in your vision, take consistent action, and remember that you have everything within you to make it reality. You are unstoppable."

Power Move 8
Unstoppable Connections: Building Relationships That Elevate Success

This power move will: Transform your network from a collection of contacts into a powerful web of authentic relationships that elevate both you and others around you.

In today's interconnected world, your network is your net worth. The relationships you build and nurture can open doors to opportunities, provide crucial support during challenges, and accelerate your journey to success. Unstoppable women understand that meaningful connections are not just about collecting business cards or growing a social media following—they're about creating authentic relationships that foster mutual growth, collaboration, and lasting impact.

"The quality of your life is directly related to the quality of your relationships." – Maya Angelou

Building unstoppable connections starts with authenticity. In a world where superficial networking is common, genuine relationships stand out. These are the connections that go beyond transactional exchanges to create real value for everyone involved. When you approach relationships with authenticity, generosity, and a genuine desire to help others succeed, you create a powerful network that supports your growth while allowing you to lift others as you climb.

Strategic relationship building isn't about knowing the most people—it's about knowing the right people and nurturing those relationships intentionally. Think quality over quantity.

Identify the types of connections that align with your values and goals, whether they're mentors who can guide you, peers who can collaborate with you, or newcomers you can mentor. Each relationship should serve a purpose while offering you the opportunity to add value in return.

Maintaining and nurturing relationships is just as important as building them. Regular check-ins, thoughtful gestures, and consistent support keep connections strong. Share resources, make introductions, celebrate others' successes, and be there during challenging times. Remember important details about people's lives and businesses—this personal touch shows that you value the relationship beyond its professional benefits.

Diverse connections enrich your network and expand your perspective. Seek relationships with people from different industries, backgrounds, and experiences. This diversity brings fresh ideas, challenges your thinking, and opens your eyes to new possibilities. When you build a diverse network, you create a rich ecosystem of knowledge, opportunities, and support that can help you navigate any challenge and seize unexpected opportunities.

An Unstoppable Woman's Story

Marian was a talented software developer who often worked alone, believing her skills would speak for themselves. Despite her expertise, she struggled to advance in her career until she realized the power of connections. She began attending tech meetups, joined women in tech groups, and started sharing her knowledge through speaking engagements. Through these efforts, she built relationships with industry leaders, fellow developers, and aspiring programmers. These connections led to speaking opportunities, consulting projects, and eventually, the launch of her own successful tech education company. Her network not only supported her success but also allowed her to create opportunities for other women in technology.

Write it Down

1. Who are the five most important connections in your professional life right now, and how can you strengthen these relationships?
2. What types of connections are missing from your network that could help you achieve your goals?
3. How can you add more value to your existing relationships and create opportunities for meaningful new connections?

Key Takeaways

- Authentic relationships are the foundation of a powerful network
- Quality connections matter more than quantity
- Give generously and focus on creating mutual value
- Maintain and nurture relationships consistently
- Embrace diversity in your network to expand opportunities and perspectives

My story

I remember when: At a conference, instead of trying to collect business cards, I spent time having a deep conversation with one person about our shared challenges as women in leadership. That connection led to not just a valuable mentorship, but a friendship that has enriched both our lives.

How Can I Incorporate This Power Move Into My Life?

Choose two people who inspire you or could mentor you. Reach out to one each week with a specific question or comment about their work. Set a reminder on your phone for each Wednesday to do this.

Summary

Unstoppable connections are built on authenticity, nurtured through genuine care, and maintained with intentional effort. By creating a diverse network of meaningful relationships, you establish a support system that can help you overcome challenges, seize opportunities, and achieve extraordinary success. Remember that every connection has the potential to change your life or someone else's — approach each relationship with purpose, generosity, and authenticity.

Unstoppable Woman's Affirmation- Say It Out Loud

"I build authentic and meaningful connections that enrich my life and career. I approach relationships with generosity, integrity, and genuine care. My network grows stronger each day as I give value and support to others. Through these connections, I create opportunities for mutual success and growth. I am connected, supported, and unstoppable."

Words from Marsha

"Your network is your greatest asset in business and in life. But remember—it's not just about who you know, it's about how deeply you connect and how much value you bring to each relationship. When you focus on building authentic connections and supporting others' success, you create a powerful community that will lift you higher than you could ever go alone."

3-Step Process:

- **Identify Your Tribe** – Recognize the people who support and uplift you.
- **Build Authentic Relationships** – Focus on building trust and meaningful connections.
- **Give and Receive** – Offer value to others while being open to receiving help in return.

Unstoppable Woman – Take Action – Your Turn:

- **Reflect:** Who in your life empowers you to be your best? How can you connect more with them?
- **Take Action:** Reach out to someone today to strengthen or build a connection.
- **Accountability:** Set a goal to meet a new person or deepen an existing relationship this week.

Be "You" Unstoppable Woman

"Every connection you make has the potential to change your life or someone else's. Don't underestimate the power of authentic relationships and genuine support. Your unique perspective, experiences, and talents are valuable to others—share them generously. When you build meaningful connections and nurture them with care, you create a network that makes you truly unstoppable."

Power Move 9
Unstoppable Learning: Growing Every Day to Reach New Heights

This power move will: Break you free from the trap of stagnation by igniting a passion for continuous growth that keeps you relevant and ahead of the curve.

Let's talk about something that's going to keep you ahead of the game - never stopping learning. In today's fast-moving world, standing still means falling behind. But here's the good news: every day brings a new chance to learn something that could change your game completely. When you commit to learning, you're really committing to becoming unstoppable.

"The more that you read, the more things you will know. The more that you learn, the more places you'll go." – Dr. Seuss

Learning isn't just about sitting in a classroom or getting another degree. It's about staying curious, asking questions, and being open to new ideas. Maybe it's listening to a podcast during your morning walk, reading industry blogs on your lunch break, or taking an online course in your pajamas. The way you learn doesn't matter as much as making sure you keep learning something new every single day.

Think of learning like going to the gym for your brain. Just like you work out to stay healthy and strong, you need to exercise your mind to keep it sharp and ready for new challenges. The most successful people I know are always learning - they're reading books, trying new things, and asking questions. They know that in today's world, what worked yesterday might not work tomorrow, so they stay ready for change by constantly updating their knowledge and skills.

But here's the thing about learning - you've got to make it work for you. If you hate reading, maybe audiobooks are your thing. If you can't sit still for long lectures, try hands-on workshops or quick video tutorials. The key is finding ways to learn that fit your style and schedule. When learning feels good, you'll want to do more of it.

One of the best ways to learn is from other people's experiences. Find mentors who've been where you want to go. Join groups where people share their knowledge. Listen to their stories - both their successes and their failures.

Technology has made learning easier than ever. You can take courses from top universities while sitting on your couch, join virtual masterminds with people from around the world, or learn a new skill through YouTube tutorials. Take advantage of these tools.

Remember, learning isn't just about adding new skills - it's about growing as a person. When you learn something new, you build confidence. You see things differently. You become more valuable to your team, your clients, and yourself. Every new thing you learn is like adding another tool to your success toolkit.

An Unstoppable Woman's Story

Lisa started as a receptionist at a small marketing firm. Instead of just doing her job, she got curious about everything happening around her. She watched YouTube videos about digital marketing during her lunch breaks. She asked the graphic designers to teach her the basics of their software. She took free online courses about social media management at night. Within two years, she had enough knowledge to move into a junior marketing role. Today, she runs her own digital marketing agency, and she still learns something new every single day. She says her success secret is simple: "I never stop being a student of my craft."

Write it Down

1. What's one skill you could learn right now that would make a big difference in your work or life?
2. How do you learn best? (Reading, watching, doing, listening?)
3. What's stopping you from learning something new, and how can you overcome these obstacles?

Key Takeaways

- Learning keeps you relevant and ready for new opportunities
- Find ways to learn that work for your style and schedule
- Learn from others' experiences and mistakes
- Use technology to make learning easier and more accessible
- Every new skill makes you more valuable and confident

My Story

Learning has always been my compass, guiding me forward no matter where I am in life. Even during my career as a professor, teaching writing and inspiring others was only one part of the journey. I was equally committed to being a lifelong learner, knowing that growth never truly stops. I loved expanding my own skills and knowledge, exploring new ideas, and challenging myself to improve, both inside and outside of the classroom.

I've seen how embracing learning with an open mind and a willing heart can lead to incredible growth, and this mindset is one I carry with me every day. Through the power of learning, I've found strength, inspiration, and purpose. It's one of the reasons I'm so passionate about empowering others to stay curious and keep evolving.

How Can I Incorporate This Power Move Into My Life?

Pick one skill you want to improve. Spend 15 minutes 3 days out of the week learning about it - whether through YouTube videos, articles, or online courses. Do this during your lunch break or right after dinner.

Summary

Learning is a lifelong journey and one of the most powerful tools you have to shape your future. By committing to ongoing growth, you empower yourself to adapt, innovate, and excel in every area of life. Knowledge gives you the courage to face new challenges, the insight to make wise choices, and the skill to continually improve. Embrace each lesson, seek knowledge with passion, and remember that every step in learning brings you closer to your dreams.

Unstoppable Woman's Affirmation-Say It Out Loud

"I am committed to lifelong learning. Every lesson I embrace opens doors to new possibilities, bringing me closer to my true potential. I am empowered by knowledge and strengthened by growth."

Words from Marsha

"Your mind is a powerful asset, and learning is the fuel that keeps it thriving. Every new idea, every piece of wisdom, and every skill you gain helps you become a more resilient and empowered version of yourself. Don't wait for the perfect moment to learn—embrace it now. Let your curiosity guide you, and remember that knowledge isn't just for the mind; it fuels your spirit and ignites your path forward. Keep learning, and keep becoming the unstoppable woman you were meant to be."

3-Step Process:

- **Identify Your Tribe** – Recognize the people who support and uplift you.
- **Build Authentic Relationships** – Focus on building trust and meaningful connections.
- **Give and Receive** – Offer value to others while being open to receiving help in return.

Unstoppable Woman – Take Action – Your Turn:

- **Reflect:** Who in your life empowers you to be your best? How can you connect more with them?
- **Take Action:** Reach out to someone today to strengthen or build a connection.
- **Accountability:** Set a goal to meet a new person or deepen an existing relationship this week.

Be "You" Unstoppable Woman

Learning isn't just about acquiring knowledge; it's about evolving into the best version of yourself. You are a constant work in progress, and that's something to celebrate. You have the power to shape your future by dedicating yourself to growth, one small lesson at a time. The beauty of learning is that it's an ongoing process. No matter how much you know today, there is always more to discover and apply

Power Move 10
Unstoppable Wins: Celebrating Every Victory on Your Journey

This power move will: Shift your perspective on success by teaching you to recognize and celebrate progress at every step, building momentum through both small victories and major achievements.

Let's talk about something we often forget to do - celebrating our wins, big and small. You know that feeling when you've crushed a goal you set for yourself? That's worth celebrating! Too many of us rush from one accomplishment to the next without stopping to acknowledge how far we've come. But here's the truth: celebrating your wins isn't just about patting yourself on the back - it's about building the confidence and momentum to keep pushing forward.

"Success is the sum of small efforts, repeated day in and day out." – Robert Collier

Think about it - every big success story started with small wins. Landing that dream client? It started with one good pitch. Building a successful business? It began with one brave decision to start. Running a marathon? It started with that first mile. When you learn to celebrate these smaller victories, you build the confidence to tackle bigger challenges. It's like putting fuel in your tank for the journey ahead.

Here's something I've learned: success leaves clues. When you take time to celebrate your wins, you're also taking time to understand what worked. Maybe it was your preparation, your persistence, or the way you handled a tough situation. These insights are gold - they show you what you're capable of and give you a blueprint for future success.

But let's get real - some days, the wins might feel small. Maybe you finally cleared your inbox, had a productive meeting, or stuck to your morning routine. Guess what? Those count too! Every small victory adds up to create unstoppable momentum. It's like building a wall brick by brick - each small win is another brick in your foundation of success.

Celebrating doesn't mean you have to throw a party every time you check something off your to-do list (though if that's your style, go for it!). Sometimes it's as simple as taking a moment to acknowledge your progress, sharing your success with a friend, or treating yourself to something special. The key is to make celebration a habit - to train your brain to recognize and appreciate progress.

Here's something else that's important: learn to celebrate others' wins too. When you cheer on your colleagues, friends, and even competitors, you create an atmosphere of success. Plus, it just feels good to be someone who lifts others up.

Remember, every win, no matter how small, is proof that you're moving in the right direction. They're like breadcrumbs on your path to bigger goals. When you acknowledge and celebrate these victories, you're telling yourself and the world that you're serious about your success.

An Unstoppable Woman's Story

Kim used to beat herself up for not achieving her goals fast enough. One day, she started keeping a "wins journal" - writing down three wins every single day, no matter how small. Some days it was big stuff like landing a new contract. Other days it was simple things like making all her calls or trying a new approach with a difficult client. After six months, she looked back at her journal and was amazed at how far she'd come. Those small daily wins had added up to major progress in her business and her confidence. Now she says celebrating her daily wins is as important as her morning coffee - it's essential fuel for her success.

Write it Down

1. What three wins (big or small) have you had this week that you haven't properly celebrated?
2. How can you build celebration into your daily or weekly routine?
3. What's your favorite way to acknowledge and celebrate your progress?

Key Takeaways

- Every win, big or small, deserves recognition
- Celebrating builds confidence and momentum
- Success leaves clues - learn from your wins
- Make celebration a daily habit
- Lift others up by celebrating their wins too

My story

I remember when: I started keeping a "wins journal" where I wrote down one achievement each day, no matter how small. Over time, those small victories added up to show me just how far I'd come.

How Can I Incorporate This Power Move Into My Life

 Keep a small notebook by your bed. Every night before sleep, write down one thing you did well that day. It can be as simple as "made a healthy lunch" or as big as "landed a new client."

Summary

Being unstoppable means never stopping learning. It's about staying curious, being open to new ideas, and constantly growing your skills. When you commit to learning something new every day, you're investing in yourself and your future. You're making sure you're ready for whatever opportunities come your way. Remember, in a world that's always changing, the person who keeps learning is the one who keeps winning.

Unstoppable Woman's Affirmation- Say It Out Loud

"I am a lifelong learner, growing stronger and smarter every day. I stay curious and open to new ideas. Every challenge is a chance to learn something new. My mind is ready to grow, my heart is open to change, and my future is bright because I never stop learning. I am unstoppable."

Words from Marsha

"Don't ever let anyone tell you it's too late to learn something new. Every day brings a fresh chance to grow, to understand more, to become better. The world is your classroom, and life is your greatest teacher. Stay curious, stay hungry for knowledge, and watch how far you can go."

3-Step Process:

- **Celebrate Every Win** – Recognize all progress, no matter how small.
- **Reflect on Your Success** – Pause to appreciate what you've accomplished.
- **Amplify Your Wins** – Share your victories with others to inspire and motivate.

Unstoppable Woman – Take Action – Your Turn:

- **Reflect:** What's one win you're proud of, big or small? How did it feel?
- **Take Action:** Celebrate your wins today—treat yourself, share with a friend, or acknowledge your success.
- **Commit:** Keep a daily log of your wins to remind yourself of how far you've come.

Be "You" Unstoppable Woman

"You've got everything it takes to learn whatever you set your mind to. Don't worry about being perfect - focus on making progress. Every little bit of knowledge adds up. Keep learning, keep growing, and keep pushing forward. That's what makes you unstoppable. Your desire to learn is your superpower - use it every single day."

Power Move 11
Unstoppable Wealth: Building Your Financial Freedom

This power move will: Transform your relationship with money from one of anxiety or avoidance to one of confidence and empowerment, giving you the tools to build lasting financial freedom.

Let's get real about money. Not just making it, but growing it, managing it, and using it to create the life you want. Financial freedom isn't just about having a fat bank account - it's about having choices, security, and the power to make decisions on your own terms. When you're financially strong, you become unstoppable in every other area of your life too.

"Don't work for money; make money work for you." – Robert Kiyosaki

Here's the truth that nobody talks about enough: money is a tool, not a goal. Think of it like a hammer - it's not about having the hammer, it's about what you can build with it. Whether you want to start a business, buy a home, travel the world, or just sleep better at night knowing you're secure, getting smart about money is your ticket to getting there.

Let's break down what building real wealth looks like. First, it's about making money - whether that's through your job, your business, or your investments. But here's the key: it's not just about how much you make, it's about how much you keep and how hard that money works for you. Ever heard the phrase "make money while you sleep"? That's what we're aiming for.

Building wealth starts with the basics. You need to know your numbers - what's coming in, what's going out, and where every dollar is going. I know, tracking expenses isn't sexy, but neither is being broke. Once you get clear on your money situation, you can start making better decisions. It's like getting on a scale when you want to lose weight - you need to know your starting point.

Here's something I learned the hard way: having multiple streams of income isn't just nice to have - it's essential. Think about it like having backup generators. If one source of power goes out, you've got others keeping the lights on. Maybe it's a side hustle, rental income, investments, or something else. The point is, don't put all your eggs in one basket.

Investing isn't just for Wall Street types. Whether it's stocks, real estate, your own business, or something else, your money should be working as hard as you do. Start small if you need to, but start somewhere. The earlier you begin, the more time your money has to grow. And remember, investing in yourself - your skills, your knowledge, your business - often gives the best returns.

Let's talk about debt. Not all debt is bad - some debt can help you build wealth, like a mortgage on a property that appreciates. But consumer debt? That's like having a hole in your pocket. Getting rid of high-interest debt should be a top priority. Every dollar you're not paying in interest is a dollar that can work for you instead

An Unstoppable Woman's Story

Rachel started as a teacher making $45,000 a year, barely making ends meet. Instead of accepting that as her financial destiny, she got serious about money. She started budgeting, cut unnecessary expenses, and used that money to pay off her credit cards. Then she started a small tutoring business on the side. She invested her extra income in low-cost index funds and eventually bought a small rental property. Five years later, she had three income streams: her teaching job, her growing tutoring business, and rental income. Now she's financially secure and teaching other women how to do the same. Her secret? "I stopped making excuses and started making plans."

Write it Down

1. What are your current income streams, and what new ones could you create?
2. What's one financial habit you need to change to build more wealth?
3. What's your biggest money goal for the next year, and what steps will get you there?

Key Takeaways

- Financial freedom gives you choices and security
- Multiple income streams create stability
- Invest early and regularly - in yourself and your money
- Good debt can build wealth; eliminate bad debt
- Know your numbers and make them work for you

My story

I remember when: I finally faced my financial fears by sitting down with all my statements and creating my first real budget. That moment of clarity, though initially overwhelming, became the foundation for building true financial independence.

Throughout my life, I've seen the incredible impact of persistence and growth, especially when it comes to wealth—not just in terms of finances but in creating a life that's rich with purpose and fulfillment. Building a solid foundation, putting in the time, and consistently showing up for what matters has been a guiding force in my journey. I've learned that wealth isn't just about money; it's about the abundance of experiences, knowledge, and connections we create along the way.

How Can I Incorporate This Power Move Into My Life

Every payday, automatically transfer a fixed amount (even if it's just $20) to a separate savings account. Then spend 5 minutes reviewing your spending from the last two weeks to find one unnecessary expense you can cut.

Summary

Building unstoppable wealth isn't about getting rich quick - it's about making smart choices consistently over time. It's about creating multiple streams of income, investing wisely, and using money as a tool to build the life you want. When you get serious about your finances, you become unstoppable in every area of your life.

Unstoppable Woman's Affirmation- Say It Out Loud

"I am smart with my money and confident in building wealth. I create multiple streams of income and make my money work for me. I invest in myself and my future. My financial decisions today create freedom and security tomorrow. I am financially savvy and unstoppable."

Words from Marsha

"Your relationship with money shapes every other area of your life. Don't be afraid to talk about it, learn about it, and get good at managing it. Financial freedom isn't just about the money - it's about having the power to choose your own path. You deserve that freedom, and you're capable of creating it."

3-Step Process:

- **Shift Your Money Mindset** – Believe that wealth is available to you.
- **Build Multiple Streams** – Diversify your income and look for opportunities.
- **Invest in Yourself** – Allocate resources to enhance your skills and wealth-building potential.

Unstoppable Woman – Take Action – Your Turn:

- **Reflect:** What are your current beliefs about wealth? How can you shift them?
- **Take Action:** Identify one new way to increase your income today (side hustle, investment, etc.).
- **Commit:** Create a plan to improve your financial situation, starting with small steps.

Be "You" Unstoppable Woman

"Your financial future is in your hands, and you have what it takes to build real wealth. Start where you are, use what you have, and keep learning as you go. Don't compare your chapter 1 to someone else's chapter 20. Focus on progress, not perfection. When you take control of your money, you become truly unstoppable. Your future self will thank you for starting today!

Power Move 12
Unstoppable Momentum: Keeping Your Fire Burning Bright

This power move will: Give you the tools to maintain your drive and enthusiasm even when facing obstacles, turning consistent action into unstoppable forward progress.

This is it - the secret sauce that keeps you moving forward when others give up. Momentum isn't just about moving fast; it's about moving forward consistently, no matter what life throws at you. When you master momentum, you become truly unstoppable. Let's talk about how to keep that fire burning bright, day after day, year after year.

**"Success isn't always about greatness. It's about consistency. Consistent hard work leads to success. Greatness will come."
– Dwayne Johnson**

Here's the truth about momentum: it's not about those days when you feel like you could conquer the world (though those are great!). It's about what you do on the days when you don't feel motivated at all. It's about building routines and habits that carry you forward, even when your motivation tank is running on empty.

Think of momentum like rolling a snowball down a hill. At first, it takes a lot of effort to get it moving. But once it starts rolling, it picks up speed and gets bigger all on its own. That's what we're aiming for in your life and business - creating that unstoppable force that keeps building on itself.

The secret to maintaining momentum is what I call your "non-negotiables" - those daily actions that you commit to no matter what. Maybe it's your morning routine, your daily planning session, or your weekly goal review. These aren't just tasks; they're the building blocks of your success. When you honor these commitments to yourself, you build trust in your own ability to follow through.

Let's get real about energy management. You can't sprint forever - trust me, I've tried! Sustainable momentum is about knowing when to push hard and when to rest. It's about working in cycles, like an athlete who knows that recovery is just as important as training. Build regular breaks into your schedule. They're not a sign of weakness; they're a strategy for lasting success.

Your thoughts create your reality. When you expect good things to happen, when you look for opportunities instead of obstacles, you create momentum in your mind that carries over into everything you do. The game-changer? Tracking your progress. When you can see how far you've come, it gives you the energy to keep going. Keep a success journal, take regular photos of your progress, or track your key metrics - whatever works for you.

An Unstoppable Woman's Story

Angel built a seven-figure business while raising three kids as a single mom. Her secret wasn't working 24/7 or having some brilliant master plan. Instead, she focused on consistent, deliberate action. Every Sunday, she planned her "power hours" for the week - those precious pockets of time when she could work on her business. She kept a "momentum journal" where she tracked her daily wins and progress. Even on her hardest days, she committed to doing just one thing to move forward. "It wasn't about making huge leaps," she says. "It was about taking small steps every single day, trusting that they would add up to something amazing." And they did.

Write it Down

1. What are your non-negotiables - the daily actions that keep you moving forward?
2. How do you recharge when your energy is low?
3. What systems can you put in place to track and celebrate your progress?

Key Takeaways

- Consistency matters more than intensity
- Build strong daily habits that carry you forward
- Balance push and recovery for sustainable success
- Track your progress to fuel your momentum
- Your mindset shapes your momentum

My story

I remember when: During a particularly challenging project, I developed a morning routine that helped me maintain my energy and focus. Even on the hardest days, that routine became my anchor, keeping me moving forward when I felt like giving up. Moving with purpose and consistency has been key to achieving my goals and finding joy in the journey. Today, I'm more passionate than ever about helping others build their own unstoppable momentum.

How Can I Incorporate This Power Move Into My Life?

Write down your most important task for tomorrow before you go to bed. Do that task first thing in the morning, before checking emails or social media. This builds momentum for your entire day.

Summary

Unstoppable momentum isn't about never slowing down - it's about always moving forward, even if it's just one small step at a time. It's about building habits that support your success, managing your energy wisely, and keeping your eyes on the prize. When you master momentum, you become unstoppable not just for a day or a week, but for life.

Unstoppable Woman's Affirmation- Say It Out Loud

"I am building unstoppable momentum every single day. My consistent actions create powerful results. I trust in my journey and celebrate my progress. Each step forward builds my confidence and strength. I am focused, I am determined, and I am unstoppable."

Words from Marsha

"This is where it all comes together. Everything we've talked about - your vision, your connections, your learning, your celebrations, your wealth - they all create momentum in your life. Keep showing up, keep pushing forward, keep believing in yourself. The world needs your gifts, your passion, and your unstoppable spirit."

3-Step Process:

- **Start Small** – Take the first step to build momentum.
- **Stay Consistent** – Keep moving forward, even when it feels slow or difficult.
- **Celebrate Your Progress** – Acknowledge the momentum you've built and keep the energy going.

Unstoppable Woman – Take Action – Your Turn:

- **Reflect:** When did you last experience momentum? What helped you keep moving?
- **Take Action:** Do something today to build momentum, whether it's completing a task or making progress on a goal.
- **Commit:** Plan to take consistent action every day for the next 7 days to build unstoppable momentum.

Be "You" Unstoppable Woman

"This is your moment. Your time to shine. Your chance to create the life you've always dreamed of. Remember, being unstoppable isn't about being perfect - it's about being persistent. It's about getting up one more time than you fall. It's about believing in yourself when nobody else does. You have everything you need right now to start building momentum toward your dreams.

Don't wait for the perfect moment - create it. Don't wait for permission - claim your power. Don't wait for someone else to believe in you - believe in yourself first. Your journey to becoming unstoppable starts with one step, one decision, one moment of courage.

You are stronger than you know, more capable than you imagine, and more unstoppable than you've ever dreamed. Keep moving forward, keep building momentum, and keep shining your light. The world is waiting for your unique magic.

Now go out there and be unstoppable!"

Resources

As you continue your journey to becoming an unstoppable woman, remember that support and inspiration are always within reach. The resources on this page are handpicked to empower you with insights, practical strategies, and a supportive community.

Whether you're looking for further reading, training, or just a daily dose of motivation, these tools are here to help you achieve your goals and keep moving forward. Explore, grow, and keep building the life you envision. Explore these resources for ongoing inspiration, tools, and insights to support your unstoppable journey!

Recommended Reads

Here are some powerful books that align with the themes of empowerment, self-development, and personal success:

- **"Atomic Habits" by James Clear** A practical guide on breaking bad habits and developing new ones. James Clear dives into the science of habit formation to help you create lasting change.

- **"Dare to Lead" by Brené Brown**
  This inspiring read dives into authentic leadership and the courage it takes to show up as yourself. Brené Brown explores vulnerability, courage, and trust as the foundations for leading a fulfilled and empowered life.
- **"The Power of Now" by Eckhart Tolle**
  This classic offers insights on mindfulness and presence, helping you to embrace each moment and find deeper peace and purpose.

Courses & Training with Marsha Lynn Hudson

Visit https://marshalynnhudson.podia.com for tools and strategies to enhance your skills and mindset in areas like personal growth, leadership, and goal-setting.

Join My Community on Facebook

Let's stay connected! Join me on Facebook for daily motivation, resources, and discussions with other like-minded women.

Access My Lead Magnet Vault

Looking for quick resources to get started or gain new insights? Visit marshalynnhudson.com to access my vault and get exclusive downloads designed to support your growth.

The 28 Day "Unstoppable Woman" Challenge

Day 1: *Set Your Intention*

Write down one main goal you want to achieve this month. Keep it visible as your daily reminder.

Day 2: *Morning Gratitude*

List three things you're grateful for. Let this be the first thing you do each morning to start with a positive mindset.

Day 3: *Affirm Your Power*

Write or say a personal affirmation that uplifts you. Start with "I am unstoppable because…"

Day 4: *Breathe and Reset*

Take five deep breaths, focus on calmness. This is a simple way to reset whenever you need it.

Day 5: *Envision Your Best Self*

Take five minutes to visualize yourself living the life you want. See yourself succeeding and feeling fulfilled.

Day 6: *Small Wins*

Write down one small achievement from the past week, however small, and celebrate it!

Day 7: *Self-Care Break*

Take 10 minutes to do something just for you—a quick walk, listen to your favorite song, or read a few pages of a good book.

Day 8: *Declutter One Space*

Pick one small area (a drawer, a shelf) and organize it. Clear space brings clear thoughts.

Day 9: *Reconnect with Your Purpose*

Write down why your goal matters to you. Remind yourself of the purpose behind your dreams.

Day 10: *Reach Out*

Connect with someone who inspires you, even if it's just a quick message to say hello.

Day 11: *Read for Growth*

Read a motivational quote or an inspiring article. Give yourself a boost of encouragement.

Day 12: *Set a Mini-Goal*

Identify a small step you can take toward your main goal today. Small steps create big progress.

Day 13: *Self-Compassion Check*

Write down one thing you appreciate about yourself. Be kind to yourself and recognize your strengths.

Day 14: *Reflect on Wins*

Review the progress you've made over the past two weeks. Write down at least two things you're proud of.

Day 15: *Set a New Intention*

Adjust or add to your goal if needed. Stay flexible and open to growth.

Day 16: *Affirm Your Strengths*

Say an affirmation aloud. Examples: "I am capable," or "I am strong and determined."

Day 17: *Plan Tomorrow's Step*

Write down one thing you'll focus on tomorrow to keep your momentum going.

Day 18: *Gratitude Check*

List three new things you're grateful for today. Gratitude keeps your outlook positive.

Day 19: *Step Outside*

Take a quick 5-minute walk outside, breathing in fresh air and resetting your mind.

Day 20: *Write Down a Dream*

Write out one big dream you have for yourself. Don't hold back— let it be a vision that excites you.

Day 21: *Compliment Yourself*

Give yourself a compliment today. Focus on something you genuinely like about yourself.

Day 22: *List Your Resources*

Write down three resources or strengths you have that will help you reach your goals.

Day 23: *Forgive and Let Go*

Think of one thing you need to release, whether it's a mistake, regret, or past hurt. Let it go with love.

Day 24: *Imagine Success*

Visualize achieving your goal. Imagine how it feels, what it looks like, and who you're with.

Day 25: *Set a Personal Boundary*

Decide on one small boundary that will protect your time, energy, or peace. Stick to it.

Day 26: *Celebrate Yourself*

Celebrate your growth over the past 26 days. Reflect on how far you've come and be proud.

Day 27: *One Last Mini-Goal*

Choose one small step you can take today that moves you closer to your goal.

Day 28: *Commit to Your Journey*

Write a short statement of commitment to yourself. Read it aloud as you finish this challenge, knowing you are unstoppable!

Stay Connected with Marsha Lynn Hudson

LinkedIn https://www.linkedin.com/in/marshalynnhudson

Facebook https://www.facebook.com/marshalynnhudson

https://www.facebook.com/marshalynnhudsonbrandstrategist/

Instagram
https://www.instagram.com/marshalynnhudsonmedia/

Youtube https://www.youtube.com/@MarshaLynnHudson

Email Marsha

marshahudsontraining@gmail.com

marsha@marshalynnhudson.com

www.marshahudsonmedia.com

Marsha's Podcast

https://podcasters.spotify.com/pod/show/marketingonlinewithease